Sherlock Holmes and the Mystery of Boscombe Pool

SIR ARTHUR CONAN DOYLE

Level 3

Retold by J. Y. K. Kerr
Series Editors: Andy Hopkins and Jocelyn Potter

Pearson Education Limited
Edinburgh Gate, Harlow,
Essex CM20 2JE, England
and Associated Companies throughout the world.

ISBN-13: 978-0-582-41698-7
ISBN-10: 0-582-41698-1

Sherlock Holmes and the Mystery of Boscombe Pool was first published as
'The Boscombe Valley Mystery' in *The Adventures of Sherlock Holmes* in 1892
This adaptation first published by Penguin Books 1991
Published by Addison Wesley Longman Limited and Penguin Books Ltd. 1998
New edition first published 1999

9 10 8

Text copyright © J.Y. K. Kerr 1991
Illustrations copyright © David Cuzik 1991
All rights reserved

The moral right of the adapter and of the illustrator has been asserted

Design by D W Design Partnership Ltd
Typeset by RefineCatch Limited, Bungay, Suffolk
Set in 11/14pt Monotype Bembo
Printed in China
SWTC/08

Published by Pearson Education Limited in association with
Penguin Books Ltd., both companies being subsidiaries of Pearson Plc

For a complete list of titles available in the Penguin Readers series please write to your local
Pearson Education office or contact: Penguin Readers Marketing Department,
Pearson Education, Edinburgh Gate, Harlow, Essex, CM20 2JE.

Contents

Introduction

'Everything points to the fact that the young man is guilty, does it not?'
I said.

'The facts are not always what they seem,' answered Holmes. 'If we look at them in another way, they can tell quite a different story.'

As usual, Sherlock Holmes has asked his friend Dr Watson to come with him to study another crime. As usual, it is Dr Watson who tells the story. A rich man, Charles McCarthy, is dead. He died near Boscombe Pool, hit on the head with something heavy. Who killed him? The police are sure that they know. Young Patience Moran saw Mr McCarthy and James, his son, by the lake. They were both shouting. James was very angry. He was lifting up his arm . . .

The facts are clear. But Sherlock Holmes is not so sure. The police have taken James away and he is in prison, waiting for the case to come to court. Holmes has to work fast to find the real murderer.

Arthur Conan Doyle was born in Edinburgh, Scotland, in 1859, one of seven children. He was a clever boy, who loved reading. After school he studied medicine at Edinburgh University. One of the teachers there was a doctor called Joseph Bell. Bell could look at a person and tell you what his job was. He had a scientific way of studying people's faces, movements and clothes. When Conan Doyle was writing about his great detective, he remembered Joseph Bell. Like Sherlock Holmes, Bell was tall and thin.

After he finished his studies, Conan Doyle first worked as a ship's doctor. Then he went to work in the south-west of England, near Portsmouth. He lived there for eight years. For part of this time, his younger brother, Innes, lived with him. Some people say that Conan Doyle used Innes for Dr Watson in his stories. Conan Doyle did not have much medical work, so he spent a lot of his time writing. His first book about Sherlock Holmes was *A Study in Scarlet*, which he wrote in 1887. He sent it to two companies but they sent the book back. A third company accepted it but paid Conan Doyle only £25! *The Sign of Four* came out three years later. But Conan Doyle's real success with Sherlock Holmes began in 1891 when he started to write short stories for the *Strand Magazine*. Later, these stories came out as complete books: first, *The Adventures of Sherlock Holmes* (1892) and then *The Memoirs of Sherlock Holmes* (1894).

Conan Doyle began to get tired of his detective and wanted to 'kill' him. In one story, Holmes had a fight with his greatest enemy, Professor Moriarty, and fell to his death in the Swiss mountains. Conan Doyle was unhappy that readers didn't show the same interest in his historical books like *The White Company* (1891) or his scientific adventure stories like *The Lost World* (1912). Everybody still preferred Holmes and Watson. Conan Doyle found that he had to bring Holmes back to life and write five more books about him. Each of these was an immediate success. In his later life, Conan Doyle became interested in sending and receiving messages to and from the world of the dead. He died in 1930, at the age of 71.

Conan Doyle was not the first person to write detective stories. He got the idea from one of his favourite writers, the American, Edgar Allan Poe. But Poe's French detective, Dupin, is almost unknown because Poe wrote only one short story about him, 'The Murders in the Rue Morgue'. Sherlock Holmes, on the other hand, is in over a hundred stories. Today, Holmes is still the world's most famous detective and one of the most famous people in English literature. The stories are on sale in many languages. There have been many plays, films, and television programmes about him. Everyone recognizes his long, unsmiling face, his special hat and special kind of pipe. 'He is all mind and no heart,' Conan Doyle once said. But for many readers Sherlock Holmes is like a real person. Since Conan Doyle died, people have written Sherlock Holmes's life story and made museums about him and his work. People from all over the world go to see his flat at 221B Baker Street, in central London.

'Will you go?' said my wife, looking across at me.

Sherlock Holmes and the Mystery of Boscombe Pool

One morning, I was having breakfast with my wife when a telegram arrived. It was from Sherlock Holmes. It read:

Are you free for a day or two? Must go to the west of England to help with the Boscombe Pool murder. Shall be glad if you can come with me. The change will be good for us. Leaving Paddington station on the 11.15 train.

'Will you go?' said my wife, looking across at me.

'I really don't know what to say,' I answered. 'I have a lot of sick people to visit.'

'Anstruther can do your work for you. You are looking tired and I think a change from your work will be good for you. You are always so interested in Mr Holmes's cases.'

'As always, you are right, my dear. But if I do go, I must get ready immediately, because the train leaves in half an hour.'

My early life as a soldier taught me to travel with very few things. In a few minutes, I was on my way to Paddington station. There I found my old friend in his long grey coat and his favourite hat. He was walking up and down the platform.

'It is really very good of you to come, Watson,' he said. 'I need a friend like you at times like this. No one can help me as you can. Please keep two corner places and I shall buy the tickets.'

We were alone during the train journey. Holmes had a large number of newspapers with him and for much of the time he wrote and thought. Finally, he made the papers

1

'Have you heard anything about this case?' he asked.

into a very large ball and threw them away, keeping only one.

'Have you heard anything about this case?' he asked.

'No, nothing. I have not seen a newspaper for some days.'

'The London papers have not written much about it. I have read them all because I need to know all the facts. It seems to be one of those cases which looks very clear. That is why I think it will be difficult.'

'Isn't that strange?'

'Oh no. Cases which seem very easy like this one are often the hardest, I find. But just now, things look very serious for the son of the murdered man.'

'So you are sure that it is a murder?'

'Not yet. It seems to be. But I must believe nothing until I have studied all the facts. Now I shall explain in a few words what I have read.

'Boscombe Valley is near Ross in Herefordshire. A large part of the land there belongs to a Mr John Turner. He made a lot of money in Australia and returned to live in England some years ago. His neighbour, Mr Charles McCarthy, was also in Australia and lives at Hatherley, a farm which belongs to Turner. The two men first met in Australia and it is natural that they have chosen to live in the same neighbourhood. Turner is the richer man and it seems that McCarthy pays him for the use of his farm. They seem to be good friends and spend quite a lot of their time together. McCarthy has one son, who is eighteen years old, and Turner has a daughter who is about the same age. The wives of both men are dead. The two families lived quietly and did not mix much with other people. McCarthy had two servants but Turner in his big house has several more – about six. That is all I have been able to find out about these families.'

'What about the murder, then?' I asked.

'Don't hurry me, Watson. Just listen. I am coming to that.

'Last Monday, 3 June, Charles McCarthy went to the town of Ross with his servant. This was in the morning. While he was there, he told his servant to hurry because he had an important meeting with someone at three o'clock that afternoon. They drove back quickly to his house at Hatherley. Just before three o'clock, McCarthy left the farmhouse and walked down alone to Boscombe Pool. He never came back.

'It is a quarter of a mile from Hatherley Farm to Boscombe Pool and two different people saw him as he walked that way. One was an old woman but we do not know her name. The other was a manservant of Mr Turner, called William Crowder. Both people say that McCarthy was alone. The servant also says that, a few minutes after he saw McCarthy go past, he also saw his son, Mr James McCarthy, going the same way. He had a gun under his arm. The son could see his father and was following him. But Crowder, the servant, thought nothing of this until he heard of McCarthy's death later that evening.'

'You explain it all so clearly,' I said.

'I have told you to listen, dear doctor. When I have finished, you can say what you like. I shall continue.

'Another person saw the two McCarthys after William Crowder. The land around Boscombe Pool is full of trees with a little grass in the open parts beside the water. A girl of fourteen, Patience Moran, was picking flowers among the trees that afternoon. She saw Mr McCarthy and his son close to the lake. They both seemed to be very angry. She heard Mr McCarthy using strong language to his son. She saw the young man lift up his arm. He seemed ready to hit his father. She felt so frightened that she ran away. When she got home, she told her mother about the quarrel. "When I saw them, they seemed to be going to have a fight," she said. Just as she was speaking, young

Patience Moran saw Mr McCarthy and his son close to the lake.
They both seemed to be very angry.

Mr McCarthy came running up to their house. "I have just found my father by the pool," he shouted. "He is dead. We must get help." He looked very excited, without either his hat or his gun. His right hand was red with blood. Immediately, Patience's parents went with him to the pool, where they found his father's dead body lying on the grass. There were many wounds in his head, made by something thick and heavy like the wooden part of the young man's gun. They found this gun lying on the grass not far from the dead man. The police soon came and immediately held the young man for questioning, then locked him up. His case will come up in a few weeks' time.'

'Everything points to the fact that the young man is guilty, does it not?' I said.

'The facts are not always what they seem,' answered Holmes. 'We think that they all point to the same thing but, if we look at them in another way, they can tell quite a different story. It is true that the case against the young man is very serious and maybe he is in fact guilty. But there are several people who believe that he is innocent. One of these is Miss Turner, the daughter of McCarthy's neighbour. She has asked Detective Lestrade to take on the case and now Lestrade, since he cannot really say no, has asked me to help him. That is why we are hurrying along in a train instead of having a quiet breakfast at home.'

'I am afraid that the case is so clear that no one will thank you for showing what happened,' I said.

'We shall see,' my friend answered. 'We both know that Lestrade is not as clever as he thinks and I am sure that I shall notice some things which he has missed. But there is something more to tell you. When the police came to Hatherley Farm and took young McCarthy prisoner, he said, "I am deeply sorry but I am not surprised. I was expecting this."'

James McCarthy came running up to the Moran family's house and said, 'I have just found my father by the pool. He is dead.'

'Of course, that shows that he is guilty,' I said.

'In no way. In fact, he has repeated many times that he is innocent.'

'But that is hard to believe, don't you think?'

'Of course not. He cannot be so stupid that he does not realize the danger which he is in. So he cannot be surprised that he is a prisoner. Clearly he is sorry that his father is dead and that they had a quarrel. His feelings are quite natural, I think.'

'So what story does this young man have to tell?'

'You can read it here in this newspaper,' said Holmes. He gave it to me and pointed to the right page. This is what I read:

Mr James McCarthy, the son of the dead man, gave the following story: 'I was away from home for three days because I had business in Bristol. I came back only last Monday in the morning. My father was not at home when I arrived. A servant told me that he was in Ross on business. After some time, I heard the wheels of his carriage coming back. I looked out of the window and saw him walking quickly away from the house. I did not know where he was going. I then took my gun and went for a walk. I wanted to shoot some birds in the trees on the other side of Boscombe Pool. On my way, I passed William Crowder, as he has told you. But he is wrong when he says that I was following my father. I had no idea that he was in front of me. When I was about a hundred yards from the pool, I heard someone call "Cooee!" My father and I often used this call. I hurried towards the pool and found him standing there. He seemed very surprised to see me and also quite angry. He asked, "What are you doing here?" I explained, we began to talk and more angry words followed. I became angry too. I felt ready to hit him but instead I decided to leave. I know that my father gets angry very quickly, sometimes about things that are not important.

I then went back towards Hatherley Farm. After only one hundred and fifty yards, I heard a terrible scream, so I ran back to the pool again. I found my father on the ground. He was dying. There were terrible wounds on his head. I dropped my gun and held him in my arms but he died almost immediately. I stayed beside him for some minutes and then I made my way to the nearest house to ask for help. I saw no one near my father when I returned with Mr and Mrs Moran. I have no idea how he got those wounds. He was a cold man and not much liked in the neighbourhood; but I do not think that he had any enemies. That is all I know about this business.'

Questioner: Did your father say anything to you before he died?

McCarthy: His voice was very weak. He spoke a few words but I only understood something about a rat.

Questioner: What did that mean to you?

McCarthy: It meant nothing. I do not think he knew what he was saying.

Questioner: What were you talking about with your father that made him so angry?

McCarthy: I prefer not to answer.

Questioner: I must ask you to tell us.

McCarthy: It is not possible for me to tell you. Please understand that it has nothing to do with his murder.

Questioner: That is for us to decide. If you do not answer, you must realize that the case against you will be worse.

McCarthy: I do not want to speak about it.

Questioner: Is it true that the call of 'Cooee' was a call which you and your father used between you?

McCarthy: Yes, it is.

Questioner: Then why did he use it before he saw you – before he even knew of your return from Bristol?

McCarthy: I do not know.

Questioner: Did you see anything unusual when you ran back to find your father?

McCarthy: Nothing very clear.

Questioner: What do you mean?

McCarthy: I was so surprised and worried that I could think only of my father. But I remember that, as I ran towards him, I saw something on the ground to the left of me. It seemed to be a piece of grey cloth – a kind of coat, I think. When I got up, I looked for it again but it was gone.

Questioner: Do you mean that it disappeared before you went for help?

McCarthy: Yes, it was gone.

Questioner: You cannot say what it was?

McCarthy: No, I just had a feeling that there was something there.

Questioner: How far from the body?

McCarthy: About fifteen yards away.

Questioner: And how far was it from the trees?

McCarthy: About the same.

Questioner: So you think that someone took it while you were only fifteen yards away?

McCarthy: Yes, but I had my back towards it.

The questioning of McCarthy ended here.

Looking at the newspaper, I said, 'I see that the questioner has used hard words about young McCarthy. He gives importance to the fact that his father called to him before he saw him and also that he did not want to explain his quarrel with his father. He tells us to remember the strange words which the dying man spoke. All these things, he says, are very much against the son.

10

Holmes laughed softly and made himself comfortable in his corner. 'Both you and the questioner have pointed to just those things which help the young man's case most. Don't you see that you believe him to be at the same time much too clever and not clever enough? He is not very clever if he cannot explain the quarrel in some way that makes us feel sorry for him. And too clever with his strange story of the rat, and the cloth which disappeared. No, Watson, I shall study this case with the idea that what the young man says is true. We shall see where that path takes us. And now I shall not speak another word about the case until we get to Ross. We shall have lunch at Swindon and that will be in twenty minutes.' Then Holmes took a book from his pocket and sat silently, reading.

It was nearly four o'clock when we arrived at last at the pretty little town of Ross. A thin man with an ugly face was waiting for us on the platform. I knew immediately that this was Lestrade, of Scotland Yard. We drove with him to an hotel, where we took rooms.

'I have asked for a carriage,' said Lestrade, as we sat drinking a cup of tea. 'I know, Mr Holmes, that you will not rest until you have visited the place of the murder.'

'A carriage? That was kind of you,' Holmes answered, 'but because of the weather I shall not need one.'

Lestrade looked surprised. 'I do not quite understand,' he said.

'There is no wind and not a cloud in the sky. I have a packet of cigarettes to smoke and the chairs in this hotel are unusually comfortable. I do not think that I shall need the carriage tonight.'

Lestrade gave a laugh. 'I am sure that you have decided how this case will end from your study of the newspapers. It is all quite clear and it becomes clearer with every new fact. Still, one

A young woman hurried into the room. 'I have driven here to tell you this: I know that James did not do it.'

has to please a young woman and this one knows what she wants. She has heard of you and she decided to ask you to come. I told her again and again that there is nothing that you can do which I have not already done but . . . Look, here is her carriage at the door!'

As he was speaking, a young woman hurried into the room: She was one of the prettiest girls that I have ever seen in my life. Her eyes were shining, her lips open, ready to speak, and her face was pink with excitement.

She looked at each of us carefully, and then turned to my friend. 'Oh Mr Sherlock Holmes,' she said. She seemed to know immediately who he was. 'I am so glad that you have come. I have driven here to tell you this: I know that James did not do it. I know it and I want you to know it too. Please be quite sure of that fact before you start your work. I have known him since we were both little children and I know his weaknesses better than anyone. But he is too soft-hearted to hurt a fly. Anyone who really knows him must believe that he is innocent.'

'I hope that we can show that to be true, Miss Turner,' said Sherlock Holmes. 'Believe me, I shall do everything possible.'

'But you have read the facts. You have studied the problem. You must see something wrong in what people are thinking. Some way of escape. Do you not believe that he is innocent?'

'I think that probably he is.'

'There, now!' she said, throwing back her head and turning to Lestrade. 'Do you hear that? He gives me hope.'

Lestrade looked unhappy. He clearly thought that Holmes was mistaken. 'I am afraid that my friend here is only guessing,' he said.

'But he is right! I know that he is right. James and his father had many quarrels about me. Mr McCarthy wanted us to get married. I have always loved James and he loves me but we are like brother and sister. He is still young and knows very little about life and . . . and . . . I mean, naturally he did not wish to marry just yet. So there were quarrels. I am sure that this was one of them.'

'And your father?' asked Holmes. 'Did he also want you to marry James?'

'No, he was against it too. Only Mr McCarthy wanted it.' Holmes was watching her carefully and we saw that her face suddenly became a deeper pink.

'Thank you for this information,' Holmes said. 'Can I come and visit your father tomorrow?'

'I am afraid that the doctor will say no.'

'The doctor?'

'Yes, haven't you heard? My poor father has not been strong

for many years but with his sadness about this murder he has become very ill. He is in bed and Dr Willows says that his case is serious. Mr McCarthy was the only person left who knew Father in the old days in Australia – when he was in Victoria.'

'Ha! In Victoria? That is important.'

'Yes, at the mines.'

'Of course. I understand that those were the goldmines where Mr Turner made his money.'

'That is right.'

'Thank you, Miss Turner. You have been a very great help to me.'

'You will tell me tomorrow if you have any news? I expect that you will go to the prison to see James. Oh Mr Holmes, if you do go, please tell him this: I know he is innocent.'

'I will, Miss Turner.'

'I must go home now because my father needs me. He is unhappy if I leave him. Goodbye and God help you in your work.' She hurried from the room and we heard her carriage moving away down the street.

'I am surprised at you, Holmes,' said Lestrade, after keeping silent for a few minutes. 'Why do you give her hope when she is sure to lose it only too soon? I am not soft-hearted, as you know, but I think you are being unkind.'

'I believe that there is a way of saving James McCarthy,' said Holmes. 'Have you an order to see him in the prison?'

'Yes, but only for you and me.'

'Then I shall change my plans and go out. We have still got time to take a train to Hereford and see him tonight?'

'Plenty of time.'

'Then let us go. Watson, I am afraid that you will be bored but I shall only be away for an hour or two.'

I walked with them to the station and then came back alone

through the streets of the little town to our hotel. There I sat and tried to read a book. But the story was so stupid that my thoughts kept returning to the Boscombe Pool mystery. I could not follow the story. Finally, I threw the book across the room and began to think only about the happenings of the day. Perhaps this unlucky young man's words were really true? In that case, what terrible thing happened between the time that he left his father and the time that he ran back to the pool, hearing his dying screams? Something very frightening, I was sure. But what was it? Maybe the shape of the wounds had something to tell me, as a doctor. I rang the bell and asked for the weekly newspaper, which had a description of them. The wounds were in a group on the back part of McCarthy's head, on the left side. Clearly the murderer hit him from behind. This fact made James McCarthy's story easier to believe, perhaps. They were face to face during their quarrel, he said. Of course, it was also possible that James hit him when his father turned his back. Still, I decided to give Holmes this information. Then there was the strange talk of a rat when the old man lay dying. It is unusual for a dying man to use words with no meaning. Probably he was trying to explain how it all happened. But what did it mean? I thought hard, trying to find an answer to the mystery; but I could not. Then there was the grey cloth which young McCarthy saw. If this was true, then perhaps the murderer dropped it – his coat maybe – when he was running away. But the son was sitting beside his father, just a few yards away and saw no one. So every part of the case seemed to bring more problems. Lestrade's ideas did not surprise me but I believed strongly in my friend Sherlock Holmes. 'He will find new facts,' I thought to myself, 'and I need not lose hope if each new fact points to young McCarthy's innocence.'

◆

There I sat and tried to read a book. But my thoughts kept returning to the Boscombe Pool mystery. Finally I threw the book across the room.

It was late before Sherlock Holmes returned. He came back alone because Lestrade was staying at a different hotel. I told him about the head wounds, a fact which he seemed to find interesting.

'The weather seems to be staying fine,' he said. 'We don't want any rain to fall before we can look at the ground. But we must rest and be fresh for important work of this kind. I did not want to begin it after that long journey. I have seen young McCarthy.'

'And what did you learn from him?'

'Nothing.'

'Couldn't he tell you anything?'

'Nothing, as I have said. At first, I thought that he must know the name of the murderer. He wanted to save him or her – that was my idea. But now I am sure that he knows as little as we do. I must say that he is not a very intelligent young man, even if he is good-looking and also, I think, good-hearted.'

'I do not think much of his taste,' I said, 'if he really does not want to marry Miss Turner.'

'Ah, that is a long, sad story. This boy is deeply in love with her. But two years ago he did a very stupid thing. Miss Turner was still at school then and away from home. He did not know her very well. James became friendly with a woman in Bristol who worked in a bar. He married her secretly. Even now, no one knows that he is married. So think of his feelings when his father told him again and again to marry Miss Turner! He dearly want-ed to marry her but he knew that it was impossible. His father, as we now know, was a cold, hard man and James could not tell him about his wife. He has spent the last three days in Bristol with this bar woman and his father of course knew nothing about it. Remember that fact. It is very important. But something good has happened at last, because his wife has now left him. She read in the newspaper about his serious trouble and wants to have nothing more to do with him. She has written to say that she has

'I have seen young McCarthy. But now I am sure he knows as little as we do,' said Holmes.

a husband already – a sailor – and that she and James are not really married. This piece of news has made poor James a lot happier.'

'But if James is innocent, then who did the murder?'

'Ah, who? I want you to notice two important facts. The first is that the murdered man went to the pool to meet someone. This person was not his son, because his son was away from home. McCarthy did not know when his son was coming back. The second fact is that the murdered man called "Cooee!", not knowing about his son's return. Those are the two things which will help to save young James. And now let us change the subject. We shall talk no more of murders and leave all that business until tomorrow.'

18

Holmes was right: there was no rain during the night and the next day was bright and cloudless. At nine o'clock Lestrade came for us with the carriage and we left for Hatherley Farm and Boscombe Valley.

'There is serious news this morning,' said Lestrade; 'I hear that Mr Turner is dangerously ill. The doctor thinks that he is dying.'

'He is quite an old man, then?' asked Holmes.

'About sixty; but his health has been bad for some time. This business has made him really ill. He was an old friend of McCarthy's and helped him in a number of ways. I have learned that he gave him free use of Hatherley Farm.'

'Is that true? This is most interesting,' said Holmes.

'Oh yes, and he has helped him in other ways too. Everyone round here speaks of his kindness to McCarthy.'

'Really? Don't you think it strange then that McCarthy wanted his son to marry Turner's daughter? The Turners are rich and the McCarthys seem to be quite poor. We know that old Mr Turner has always been against the idea. His daughter told us that. Don't you find that McCarthy's friendliness is a little unusual?'

'You are always full of ideas, Mr Holmes,' said Lestrade, looking at me with a smile. 'I have come here to study the facts and they are difficult enough. Your thoughts always fly away from the real problems.'

'You are right,' said Holmes quietly. 'You do find it difficult to notice the facts.'

'Well, I have understood one fact which you do not seem to get hold of,' answered Lestrade, not very pleased.

'And that is?'

'That young McCarthy killed his father; any other way of seeing this case is just not possible.'

'Let us agree to disagree,' said Holmes, laughing. 'But if I am not mistaken, there is Hatherley Farm on the left.'

'Yes, that is it.'

It was a long, low building made of grey stone and it looked comfortable. But the windows were all shut and there was no smoke coming up from the roof. It looked empty. We knocked on the door and a young servant girl came out. She showed us first the boots which old Mr McCarthy was wearing at the time of his death. She also showed us a pair of the son's boots. Holmes studied their size and shape very carefully. He then asked to see the back of the house. From there we took the path which went to Boscombe Pool.

Holmes seemed to change as he hurried towards the place of the murder. He stopped being the quiet thinker of Baker Street. His face became redder and darker. His eyes shone with a hard light. He pressed his lips together and held his face down and his body low, studying the ground. His thoughts were turned so fully to the case that he did not seem to hear anything that we said. If he did, he answered only with a short word or two. He made his way quickly and silently along the path which went across the fields and then down through the trees to Boscombe Pool.

The ground was soft and wet as we got nearer. There were the marks of many feet both on the path and on the short grass on each side. Sometimes Holmes hurried on, sometimes he suddenly stood still. Once he walked away from the path into a field. Lestrade and I walked behind him. Lestrade seemed bored and uninterested in what Holmes was doing but I watched my friend carefully, knowing that every movement had a meaning.

Boscombe Pool is a small piece of water about one hundred and twenty yards wide. It lies at the end of the Hatherley Farm land where it joins the beautiful park land belonging to Mr Turner. Above the trees on the far side of the pool we could see the big red roofs of Turner's home. On the Hatherley

Holmes studied the size and shape of the boots very carefully.

Holmes ran here and there like a dog which has smelled a wild animal.

side of the pool the trees grew thick. There was a narrow piece of open ground about forty yards wide between the trees and the water of the lake. This open part was covered with short, wet grass. Lestrade showed us the place where the body was lying when they found it. In fact, the ground was so soft that I could see the marks left by McCarthy's fall. But, looking at Holmes, I realized from his excited face and the quick movement of his eyes that he was learning many other things from the marks on the grass. He ran here and there like a dog which has smelled a wild animal. Then he turned to the detective.

'Why did you go into the pool?' he asked Lestrade.

'I thought that maybe there was a gun or a piece of clothing or something like that in the water. But tell me, how. . .?'

'Oh come now, Lestrade. I have no time. That left foot of yours is everywhere. A child can see it. Look over there, where it disappears into the grass. This case was perfectly easy until a crowd of people came and stupidly walked all over the place. Here is where the Morans came and their footmarks have covered the ground for five or six yards around the body. But here are three different lines of the same feet.'

He took out a magnifying glass and lay down on top of his coat to see the marks better. Talking to himself more than to us, he said, 'These are young McCarthy's feet. Twice he was walking and once he was running fast, because his toes are pressing deeper into the ground. That follows his story, does it not? Then here are the father's footmarks as he walked up and down. What is this, then? Ha, ha! What have we here? Some-one walking on his toes. In boots with square toes too. Quite unusual boots. They come, they go, they come again – of course, that was for the coat. Now, where did they come from?'

He lay down and studied the ground with his magnifying glass.

He ran up and down, sometimes losing and sometimes finding the line of footmarks. Soon we were standing in the shadow of a very big tree, the largest of them all. Holmes followed the marks to the far side of the tree. Then he lay down on his front again with an excited shout. For a long time, he stayed there, turning over the dry leaves until he picked up something small, which looked burned. He put this into an envelope. Next, he studied both the ground and the sides of the tree with his magnifying glass. A big rough stone was lying among the leaves. He looked at this too with great interest and kept it. Then he followed another line of footmarks. These went along a path through the trees until they came to a road; where the marks disappeared.

'It has been a most interesting case,' Holmes said, becoming himself again. 'I think that this little house on the right must be the Morans' home. I will go in and have a word with Mr Moran.

24

A big rough stone was lying among the leaves. Holmes looked at this with interest and kept it.

Perhaps I will write a short letter. After that we shall drive back to the town and have lunch. Please walk to the carriage. I shall be with you again in ten minutes.'

◆

Ten minutes later, we were in the carriage, driving back to Ross. Holmes was still carrying with him the stone, found among the trees. 'You will be interested in this,' he said to Lestrade, holding it out.

'I see no marks on it.'

'There are none.'

'How do you know that it is important, then?'

'The grass was growing under it. Clearly it was lying there for only a day or two. I could not find the place that it came from: there are too many stones around. But it is the right shape to make the wounds in McCarthy's head.'

'And the murderer?'

'He is a tall man, left-handed, with a bad right leg. He wears thick shooting boots and a grey coat, smokes Indian cigars, uses a cigar-holder and carries a pocket-knife – not a very sharp one. There is more information that I can give you; but that will be enough for you to find him, I think.'

Lestrade laughed. 'I am afraid I find all this hard to believe,' he said. 'This information is all very well but it does not show that a person is guilty of murder.'

'We shall see,' said Holmes. 'You work in your way and I shall work in mine. I shall be busy this afternoon and I shall probably go back to London on the evening train.'

'And leave the case unfinished?'

'No, finished.'

'But the mystery?'

'Is a mystery no more.

'Who was the guilty person then?'

'Oh, God help us! The person I have just described, of course.'

'But who is he?'

'That will not be difficult to find out. The number of people who live in this neighbourhood is not large.'

Lestrade had a hopeless look on his face. 'I am a sensible man,' he said slowly. 'I really cannot run all over the place looking for a left-handed man with a bad leg. My friends at Scotland Yard will laugh at me.'

'All right,' said Holmes quietly. 'I have given you the information. Now here we are at your address, I believe. Goodbye. I shall send you a few words before I leave.'

We dropped Lestrade at his hotel and then drove to ours, where we found lunch upon the table.

'Look here, Watson,' said my friend when the meal was over. 'Just sit here in this chair and listen to me for a little. I am not sure what to do and your ideas will be useful. Light a cigar and I shall explain.'

'Please do.'

'Well, when we first learned about this case, there were two things that we both noticed immediately. They are both parts of young McCarthy's story. To me they showed him to be innocent. To you they seemed to make him guilty. The first thing is that his father called "Cooee" to him before he saw him. The second is that he spoke of a rat as he lay dying. He said several other words, you remember, but that was the only word that his son understood. Now these two facts must be the start of our thinking. We shall also begin by believing that the boy's story is perfectly true.'

'What about this "Cooee", then?'

'Well, clearly the father was not calling to his son. The son, as far as he knew, was in Bristol. It was just luck that James heard his father's call. The "Cooee" was for the person that old McCarthy was going to meet. But "Cooee" is a special call that Australians use. The person whom McCarthy expected to meet at Boscombe Pool was probably someone who knew Australia.'

'What about the rat, in that case?'

Sherlock Holmes took a piece of paper from his pocket and put it on the table. 'This is a map of Australia,' he said. 'I sent for it last night.' He put his hand over part of the map. 'What do you read?' he asked.

'ARAT,' I read.

'And now?' He lifted his hand.

'BALLARAT.'

'Quite right. That was the word which the old man spoke; but his son only understood the last part of it. He was trying to give the name of his murderer: Mr Something of Ballarat.'

'That's most surprising!' I said.

'It is perfectly easy,' said Holmes. 'And now, you see, the number of possible people immediately becomes much smaller. Someone who has a grey coat or jacket: that is another thing we can be sure about, if we believe the son's story. We have already come from knowing nothing to a picture of an Australian from Ballarat with a grey coat.'

'Quite true.'

'And this person felt at home in the valley, because it is only possible to get to the pool across other people's land. Strangers cannot usually go there.'

'Again you are right.'

'Then there is our visit today. By looking carefully at the ground I was able to describe the wanted man still more fully to that stupid detective Lestrade.

'But how did you find out those other facts?'

'You know my ways. It is the very small things that I always look for.'

'You knew that he was tall, because the space between the

footmarks showed a man with long legs. And the marks also told you what kind of boots he wore.'

'Yes, they were unusual boots.'

'But his bad leg?'

'The mark of his right foot was always less clear than the mark of his left. He stood more heavily on the left because his right leg hurt him.'

'But you also say that he is left-handed?'

'Ah, yes! It was you, dear Watson, who noticed the kind of head wound which the doctor described. The murderer hit McCarthy from behind but on the left side of the head. This shows that he was left-handed. Try to do it with your right hand, if you do not believe me. During the quarrel between the father and son, he stood behind that big tree. He was smoking at the time. I found the ash from a cigar, which I know to be an Indian cigar, at the foot of the tree. You remember that smoking is one of my favourite subjects and that I have written a paper on the ash from one hundred and forty different kinds of pipes, cigars and cigarettes. I looked around and soon found the cigar end lying among the leaves. It was an Indian cigar, from a shop in Rotterdam.'

'And the cigar-holder?'

'I could see that he did not put the cigar end in his mouth, so I know that he uses a cigar-holder. The end was cut off, not bitten off, but the cut was not a clean one. This showed me that he used an old pocket-knife.'

'Holmes,' I said, 'you have described this man perfectly. Now he cannot escape and you have saved an innocent man's life. Now I see where all these facts are pointing. The guilty man is . . .'

♦

'Mr John Turner,' called out the hotel waiter, opening door of our sitting-room for a visitor.

The man who came in was strange and frightening to look at. He walked slowly and with difficulty. He looked sick; but his hard face, full of deep lines, and his heavy arms and legs showed that he was strong, both in body and in his feelings. His untidy beard, thick grey hair and dark eyes gave him a wild, proud look but his face was white as ash. I noticed the light blue colour of the skin around his nose and lips. As a doctor, I could see immediately that he was seriously ill.

'Please sit down on the sofa,' said Holmes softly. 'So you got my letter?'

'Yes, Moran brought it to me. It says that you want to see me here, because it will make things easier.'

'I think that people will talk if they see me going to your house.'

'And why do you want to see me?' He looked at my friend with sad, tired eyes. He seemed already to know the answer to his question.

'Yes,' said Holmes, answering his look more than his words. 'It is true. I know all about McCarthy.'

The old man hid his face in his hands. 'God help me!' he shouted. 'I did not want the young man to get hurt. If the case goes against him, I promise you that I shall tell the police everything.'

'I am glad to hear it,' said Holmes in a serious voice.

'I have not spoken yet only because of my dear girl. Maybe I – but no, it will break her heart if she hears that I am a prisoner.'

'Perhaps that need not happen,' said Holmes.

'What?'

'I am not a policeman. I understand that it was your daughter who asked me to come, so I am working for her. But,' and here he looked hard at Turner, 'you must save young McCarthy.'

30

Holmes sat down at the table with a pen and some paper, 'Just tell us the true story,' he said.

'I am a dying man,' said Turner. 'I have had diabetes for years. My doctor does not think that I have more than a month to live. But naturally I prefer to die under my own roof than in prison.'

Holmes stood up, crossed to the table and sat down at it with a pen in his hand and some paper in front of him. 'Just tell us the true story,' he said. 'I shall write it all down. You will put your name to it and Watson here will listen to everything. Then if I need to save young McCarthy's life, I can give it to the police. I promise you that I shall not use it until I must.'

'Very well,' said the old man. 'I do not think that I shall live until the case comes up, so it does not matter much to me. But I want to save Alice's feelings if I can. It is a terrible thing for her to live with. She is so young . . . And now I will explain every-thing to you. It has taken a long time to happen but it will not take me a long time to tell. You did not know this dead man, McCarthy. He was a true criminal – bad in every possible way. I hope that you never fall into the hands of someone like him. He has sat on my back for twenty years and he has made my life impossible. I shall tell you first how I met him and became tied to him and his greedy ways.

'It was in the early '60s at the mines. I was a young man then, hot-blooded and ready to try anything new. I made some bad friends, began drinking, had no luck in finding gold. So I left the mines and became what you call here a gangster – a robber on the roads. There were six of us and we had a wild, free life, robbing a sheep station sometimes or stopping the carriages on the road to the mines. Black Jack of Ballarat was the name I took and in Australia people still remember our group as the Ballarat Boys. One day, a carriage was carrying gold from Ballarat to Melbourne, so we hid beside the road and took it by surprise. There were six guards on horses and six of us, so we nearly lost the fight. But we shot four of them within a few minutes. They killed three of our boys before we got our hands on the gold. I put my gun to the head of the driver, who was this same man, McCarthy. I meant to shoot him but decided to let him go. I still remember his greedy little eyes looking hard at my face. He planned to remember me. We rode away with the gold and became rich men. I left my old friends and made my way back to England. Here no one knew me or my past. I decided to stop travelling and live a good and quiet life. A family wanted to sell that big house at Boscombe, so I bought it. I began to put my money to good uses, unlike the way I first got it. I also got married. My wife died young but she left me dear little Alice. Alice is all the world to me. Even when she was still a baby, her little hand seemed to show me the right way to live. She is the first person who has ever done that. In a word, I changed my selfish ways and did everything I

'One day, a carriage was carrying gold from Ballarat to Melbourne,
so we hid beside the road and took it by surprise.'

could to become a better person. All was going well until McCarthy came along.

'I was in London on business one day and I met him by accident in Regent Street. He was almost without shoes on his feet or a coat on his back.

' "Here we are at last, Jack," he said, touching me on the arm. "We shall be like a family to you. There are two of us, me and my son, and you can look after us now. And if you do not – remember that this is England. There is always a policeman nearby to tell my story to."

'Well, they came down to the West Country and I could not shake them off. They lived without paying in the best farm that I had. There was no rest for me now, no forgetting. Everywhere I went, his greedy, smiling face was at my side. He asked for everything that he needed and I gave it to him without question: money, a house, a carriage. It got worse as Alice grew up. He soon realized that I was more afraid of her knowing my past than I was of the police. At last, he asked for the one thing I could not give. He asked for Alice. His son, you see, was a young man and Alice too was not a child any more. He thought it a wonderful idea for his son to have all my land and money, when he married Alice. But of course, I could not agree. I did not dislike the boy but his father's blood is in him and that is enough. I told McCarthy no – never. McCarthy was ready to go to the police. I told him to do his worst. We finally agreed to meet at the pool, half-way between our two houses. We were going to talk about McCarthy's plan one more time.

'When I went down there, I saw him talking to his son. They were having a quarrel about Alice. I hid behind a tree and smoked a cigar, because I needed to talk to Charles alone. But as I listened to his words, everything inside me that was black and angry seemed to break out. He was pressing his son to marry my daughter. It didn't seem to matter what my daughter's feelings were. He spoke of her as if she was a woman of the streets. It made me wild to think of my dearest child in the hands of that criminal. How could I break the tie? I was already a dying man with no hope left. My head was clear and my arms were still strong but I did not have long to live. But my daughter! And the picture she had of her loving father! I could save them both. I only had to stop that man's tongue from telling my secret. So I did it, Mr Holmes. I feel able to do it again, right or wrong. I have done many bad things in my life but I have paid for them. I could not stand still and see my innocent daughter so hurt. I hit him and he fell. To me he seemed nothing more than an animal. His screams brought his son running back but by this time I was among the trees. Of course, I had to go back and get my coat, which I dropped as I hurried away. That is the true story, Mr Holmes, the story of everything that happened. Now, show me that paper.'

'Well, it is not for me to speak of right or wrong,' said Holmes, as the old man wrote his name at the bottom of the last page. 'I hope that I shall never have to show that you are guilty.'

'I hope not, sir. And what do you mean to do now?'

'Because of your health, I shall do nothing. You know too well that you must live with your terrible past.' Holmes pointed to the handwritten pages on the table. 'I will keep this information and if they decide that young McCarthy is guilty of this murder, I must of course use it. If that does not happen, no man alive shall ever see it. Your secret will be safe with us. And the mystery of Boscombe Pool will stay a mystery for ever.'

'Goodbye, then,' said the old man in a broken voice. 'When your time comes, you will be able to die knowing that you have done a great kindness.'

His great sick body was shaking as he slowly left the room.

'It is not for me to speak of right or wrong,' said Holmes, as the old man
wrote his name at the bottom of the last page.

'God help us,' said Holmes, after keeping silent for some time. 'Why is life so hard on poor old men like him? Every time that I meet a case like this, I say to myself: "There but for the goodness of God goes Sherlock Holmes." '

James McCarthy's case came up some weeks later. The decision was: not guilty of murder. The few facts which Holmes gave to the police were enough to free him. Old Turner lived for seven months more but he is now dead. It seems that James and Alice will soon become husband and wife, knowing nothing of that great black cloud that rests over the past.

ACTIVITIES

Before you read

1 Look at the pictures in this part of the story.
   a When does the story happen?
     100 years ago? 50 years ago? 10 years ago?
   b Which pictures show Sherlock Holmes?

2 All these words come in the first part of the story. Choose the right meaning for each from the list a–i below.
   alone   carriage   case   guilty   innocent
   mine   quarrel   servant   telegram   wound
   a shown by law to be a criminal
   b a way of travelling before there were cars
   c somebody who works for other people in their home
   d shown by law not to be a criminal
   e a fight using words only
   f a hole or cut in the body
   g a place where men get metal out of the ground
   h a problem, e.g. a crime, that detectives have to study
   i a very quick kind of message, not used today

After you read

3 Can you name these people?
   a the murdered man
   b his neighbour, living near Boscombe Pool
   c a young man held by the police
   d a young woman, daughter of 'b' above
   e a girl who saw a family quarrel
   f a police detective
   Which two of these people are in love?

4 Why do the police think that James McCarthy is the murderer?

Before you read

5 Write sentences to show the meaning of these words from the story:

   a mark / path

   b ash / cigar / magnifying glass

6 Look at the picture on page 21.

   a What is the name of the building?

   b Why do you think that Holmes is looking at boots and shoes?

After you read

7 Copy this map of the Boscombe Valley. Then draw the movements of Sherlock Holmes on the day that he visited Boscombe Pool. Start from Hatherley Farm and finish where the carriage was waiting.

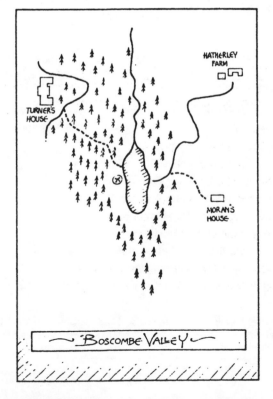

8 Holmes knows these things about the murderer:

a he is left-handed

b he smokes Indian cigars

c he has a bad right leg

Explain how Holmes finds out these facts.

Pages 30–37

Before you read

9 Can you guess the name of the murderer? Why did he or she kill Mr McCarthy? Discuss your ideas with other students.

After you read

10 How does Australia come into the story? Use just one sentence for your answer.

11 Why does Holmes decide to keep the true story of the murder from the police? Give two reasons.

Writing

12 Describe Sherlock Holmes. Write three sentences about his face, body and clothes. Then write three sentences about Holmes as a person.

13 Write a description of the murderer. Use only the facts which Holmes gives to Watson (see pages 27–29). Start your description like this:

WANTED FOR MURDER

A man . . .

14 Look at the questioning of James McCarthy on pages 9–10. Write the questioning of Patience Moran by Detective Lestrade in the same way (see page 4).

15 Write a note to a friend about this book. Say if you think that he or she will enjoy it or not and give your reasons.

Answers for the activities in this book are available from your local Pearson Education office or contact: Penguin Readers Marketing Department, Pearson Education, Edinburgh Gate, Harlow, Essex, CM20 2JE.